We are growing fast now. We
need to take good care of
ourselves. This book will tell you
all the things we do to stay
strong and healthy. If you do
them, you will be healthy, too.

1

The right foods help kids grow strong. Fruits and vegetables are good. We make healthy choices.

We eat some snacks but not many.

"How about some chips, Mom?" I ask when we shop.

She says, "Okay, but no cookies this time."

Did you know your body needs lots of water? Drink six glasses a day. It is better for you than juice and soda. Water helps to keep you healthy.

Run every day. It makes you
strong. Playing sports is a good
way to run and have some fun.
Running will make you feel great!

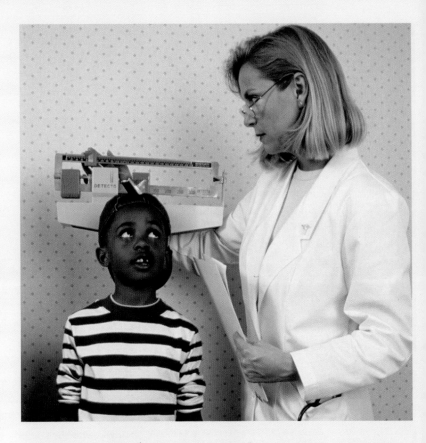

See the doctor for check-ups.
The nurse will weigh and measure
you to see how you have grown.

"My, you are big now!" she will
say.

"Yes, you are right," you can
tell her.

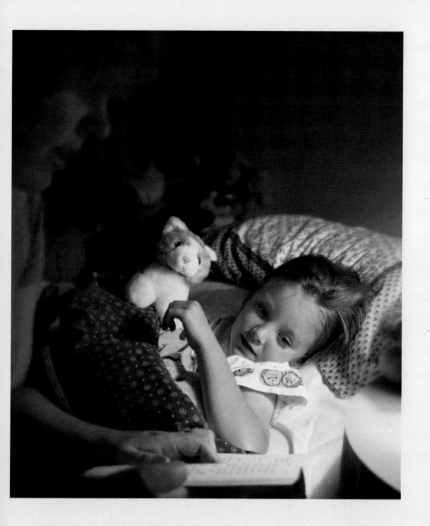

Get a good sleep every night. Being tired is no fun. When you sleep well, you will be ready for the next day. You will be strong, and you will feel good.

Our minds need to be strong, just like our bodies. We use our minds every day, no matter what we do.

Are you using your mind right now? Yes, you are. Good for you!